Benefitting from Obamacare

How one church used the ACA to their advantage

S.L. POTTS

2018 Edition

Copyright © 2017 by BROKEPASTOR LLC.

All rights reserved. No part of this work may be reproduced, stored in a retrieval system, or transmitted in any form or by any means – electronic, mechanical, photocopy, recording, or otherwise – except for brief quotations for the purpose of review or comment, without the prior permission of the author.

Requests for information should be addressed to:
admin@brokepastor.com.

This publication is designed to provide competent and reliable information regarding the subject matter covered. However, it is sold with the understanding that the author and publisher are not engaged in rendering legal, accounting, financial, or other professional advice. Laws and practices often vary state to state and country to country, and if legal or other expert assistance is required, the services of a competent professional person should be sought. The author and publisher specifically disclaim any liability that is incurred from the use or application of the contents of this book. From a Declaration of Principles jointly adopted by a Committee of the American Bar Association and a Committee of Publishers and Associations.

Original and modified cover art by Victor and CoverDesignStudio.com.

Unless otherwise noted, Scripture quotations are from the ESV® Bible (The Holy Bible, English Standard Version®), copyright © 2001 by Crossway, a publishing ministry of Good News Publishers. Used by permission. All rights reserved.

ISBN-13: 978-0-9994737-3-3

Visit our website, www.brokepastor.com.

To the dear people of Cornerstone Bible Church, past and present, who have loved us and cared for us for many years.

Table of Contents

Preface 9

Chapter 1 - Our Story 11
    A Little Context 11
    Understanding Obamacare 13
    Getting Confirmation 15
    Dropping Coverage 15
    Applying 17
    Since That Time 18

Chapter 2 - Considerations 21
    Understanding Pastoral Compensation 21
    Balancing Salary and Housing Allowance 22
    Timing 22
    Choosing a Plan 23
    Getting Counsel/Advice 23
    Increasing Compensation Over Time 24
    Non-Pastoral Employees 25

Chapter 3 - Final Thoughts 27

Preface

Let me be extremely clear from the very outset of this book: what I am about to describe in the pages that follow is not intended to be understood as a suggestion or recommendation that you should make the same decisions that we made.

In fact, as I type these words, the future of the Affordable Care Act (ACA) is unclear due to the current political climate in Washington, and neither I nor anyone else knows what will happen with this legislation in the future. That said, if things continue as they are now, there is a possibility that your church could benefit from Obamacare as our church did.

My only purpose for writing is to explain how our church used the provisions of the ACA to save well over $100,000 in medical insurance premiums over the past three years while, simultaneously, allowing our pastors to receive excellent medical coverage through Obamacare.

Please know that, before embarking on this path, we checked and double-checked our decision both internally and with our CPA, and, so far, we have had no problems. Regardless, I encourage you to read this account carefully and with discernment, and I implore you to get wise counsel from a CPA before making any decisions regarding changes to your church's medical insurance benefits.

S.L. Potts
Virginia Beach, VA
August 8, 2017

Chapter 1
Our Story

It was the summer of 2014, and the provisions of the Patient Protection and Affordable Care Act (a.k.a Affordable Care Act, ACA, and/or Obamacare) had been in effect for almost a year.

Despite President Obama's repeated promise that if you liked your plan, you could keep it, what we were hearing from our church's medical insurance provider was that the plan we liked and had used for many years was going away due to the ACA.

A Little Context

Now, I should probably back up a bit and provide some context just so you can appreciate the dilemma we were facing that summer. Up to 2014, our church had always provided full medical coverage for each full-time employee and their family at no cost to the employee.

In my case, I became the lead pastor of our church in September 2007, and was the only full-time, vocational pastor until we hired a second pastor in October 2013.

Prior to hiring our second pastor, the total monthly premium paid by the church for my family's insurance coverage was $347.48/month.[1]

---

[1] As of August 2013.

This provided us with an excellent plan with low copays and lots of options for choosing doctors.

As we prepared to bring on our second pastor, we were hoping that our total monthly costs (as a church) would simply double . . . to about $700/month. Unfortunately, the timing of our decision to hire a second pastor couldn't have been worse in this respect.

Open enrollment in the Obamacare exchanges was about to begin on October 1, 2013 . . . the exact same day our new pastor was supposed to begin his job with us. As we prepared to bring him on board, we were informed that we could not simply add him into our existing plan. Because of Obamacare, we would have to create a new group plan . . . which would mean that my family's plan and rate was going to change as well.

Imagine our shock when we received the quote for our two families' combined medical coverage costs - $1,310.27 – almost double what we were hoping for!

Not being a large church with a large budget, that cost came as quite a blow to us. However, at the time, we didn't think we had any other options, and so, we agreed to a full year of coverage at that price. As we did, we were warned by our insurance provider that our rates would likely be higher when we renewed next October, but no one knew how high they would be.

As the following summer approached, we were holding our breath waiting for notice of the impending premium increase. When it arrived, we were blown away again. It had more than doubled to $2,714.53/month for a plan that was getting less and less attractive each year.

As we crunched the numbers, we knew that there was no way our church could afford to pay over $32,000 in the coming fiscal year to provide health insurance coverage for myself and our other pastor.

What were we going to do?

Understanding Obamacare

Fearing that the increase would be as bad as it was, we had begun to do some research in order to understand the available ACA plans and subsidies early in 2014.

Most of the basic details were fairly well-known. On the individual side, everyone had to either have a compliant health insurance plan or pay a penalty. Generally speaking, if your employer offered a health plan for you, no matter how good or bad, you could not apply for coverage through the healthcare marketplace. Otherwise, you could use the exchanges. In addition, if you purchased a plan through one of the healthcare exchanges and your modified adjusted gross income (MAGI) was within 400% of the federal poverty level, you would qualify for a subsidy to help pay for your monthly premium and to (possibly) help reduce your maximum, annual, out-of-pocket, expense limit.[2]

On the business side, employers with fifty or more full-time-equivalent (FTE) employees were required to provide group coverage. For employers with fewer than fifty FTE employees, they could: A) choose to not provide coverage, B) choose to use the Small Business Health

---

[2] Both the subsidy and cost-sharing benefits are tiered benefits. See http://www.kff.org/health-reform/fact-sheet/summary-of-the-affordable-care-act/ for more information.

Options Program (SHOP) to purchase coverage, or C) continue to purchase coverage directly from an insurance provider of their choice. In addition, employers could not A) purchase coverage on behalf of an employee through an individual healthcare exchange, nor B) reimburse employees for purchasing coverage through one of the healthcare exchanges. Failure to comply with any of the requirements listed above could result in major fines for businesses.

In our case, as a church, we were well below the 50 FTE threshold.[3] Of the three options listed above that were available to us, we had chosen Option C – to purchase coverage directly from the insurance provider of our choice . . . which was going to cost us $2,714.53/month starting in October 2014. We looked into Option B, but found that the pricing in the SHOP marketplace was about the same as Option C.

At some point, we began to toy with the idea of choosing Option A – not providing any coverage at all.

This started when I signed up for a healthcare.gov account and began looking into the prices of plans available there. While signing up for an account, I was asked to provide my adjusted gross income (AGI) from our prior year's tax return.[4]

Well, if you have read one of my other books, *How to Not Be a Broke Pastor* or *Structuring Pastoral Compensation*, you know that, for income tax purposes, a pastor's housing allowance is excluded from his income.

---

[3] We had two full-time employees and one part-time employee at that time.
[4] Line 37 on form 1040.

In other words, it doesn't appear in a pastor's AGI . . . which makes a pastor appear to be poorer than he actually is (from a tax perspective) on his tax return.

In fact, when I finished submitting my account info on healthcare.gov and finally got to the screen where it showed me the plans and prices available, I was SHOCKED by what I saw!

Because my AGI was so low, I qualified for both the maximum subsidy and the maximum cost-sharing reduction. In other words, I could get a plan that was as good as, if not better than, the plan we currently had through the church for about $50/month. In addition, our maximum out-of-pocket cost for the year would only be about $1,000! I couldn't believe it. Was this for real?

Getting Confirmation

I immediately set up a meeting with our church's accountant to talk this through in detail. He did some digging and found that, sure enough, a pastor's housing allowance was not counted towards his MAGI for ACA subsidy calculation purposes. In fact, it can't be. That portion of his income is automatically free from income tax and income tax calculations.

Of course, the problem was that we could not qualify to use the healthcare exchanges since our church provided health coverage for us. As long as we were being offered medical insurance coverage through our church, we were stuck.

Dropping Coverage

I first approached the other vocational pastor of our church with what I had learned. As we worked through the information and facts together, we realized that this could actually be the answer to the church's problem.

We took our proposal to the Elder Board of our church and showed them what we had found. At first, they were both skeptical of the idea and hesitant to even consider purposefully dropping our health insurance coverage. Would it work? Was it ethical? Was there no other way?

These were not easy questions to answer. As to whether or not it would work, we felt confident that it would . . . but we didn't know of any other churches who had done the same thing. So, in a sense, we were taking a bit of a chance.

As to whether or not it was ethical, I didn't have any concerns, personally speaking. We weren't lying about anything. We weren't hiding anything. The way I saw it, it was just another weird (but beneficial) quirk in how pastors and their income are treated by the IRS.[5] Why would we not take advantage of it since it helped both us and the church?

Finally, as to whether or not there was another way, based on our projections for how much it was going to cost to provide health insurance for myself and the other pastor over the next fiscal year, there really was no way our church could afford to provide us with medical coverage . . . not without beginning to require us to pay hundreds of dollars monthly towards the overall premium.

---

[5] See *How to Not Be a Broke Pastor* or *Structuring Pastoral Compensation* to understand the many quirks and benefits related to pastoral compensation.

So, with all the facts before us, along with the reality of the impending cost increases, the Elders approved our plan, and we presented it to our membership for final approval.

Like our Elders, our members were very concerned about the idea of dropping our coverage, but they trusted us and our Elder team and voted to drop all medical coverage for all employees effective December 31, 2014, as long as we promised to come back to them if it didn't work.

While businesses or churches cannot reimburse an employee directly for buying insurance through one of the healthcare exchanges, they can always increase their income. So, to help offset the added expense, our church gave each of us a small raise.

For good or bad, we were about to become Obamacare guinea pigs!

Applying

As soon as open enrollment began that year, I officially applied for coverage. As expected, due to our low MAGI, I qualified for the largest possible premium and cost-sharing subsidies.[6]

I was so excited . . . until I read the official confirmation letter. Because our MAGI was so low, our children had been denied coverage pending a review by our local Social Services office to see if they qualified for Children's Health Insurance Program (CHIP) or a similar state-run program.

---

[6] My monthly premium was $45.98, and our maximum out-of-pocket expense limit was $1,000 for our entire family.

After some quick research, I knew that they would not qualify for either program. While Obamacare subsidies may have been based on AGI alone, these other programs would include all sources of income, including my housing allowance. This meant that they would not qualify for coverage . . . which was what we wanted anyway.[7]

Unfortunately, getting that official rejection was going to take some time, and our children could not be covered by our Obamacare policy until they were officially rejected. This was an unforeseen problem, and it caused my wife and I to become genuinely concerned about something happening to them during that in-between time while they had no coverage.

It took between 60-90 days to get that initial, official rejection letter in hand. I had to call numerous people in our local Social Services office (and make numerous visits to the office as well) to try to expedite the decision; but, eventually, they were rejected, and the kids were added to our Obamacare plan that same day. Finally, we were all covered.

SINCE THAT TIME
Since that initial start-up period, things have gone smoothly. While our premiums have still increased over time, the increases we have experienced are nothing compared to what has happened in the private sector.[8] Because the plans offered through the healthcare exchanges are the same plans available for purchase privately, we have only used major insurance providers. We have not noticed any difference in

---

[7] I should note that I know other pastors whose children are on CHIP/Medicaid, and they love it.

[8] As of 2017, I now pay $82.16/month for our insurance coverage.

terms of coverage or care between what we have now versus what we had before Obamacare.

From the church's perspective, I would estimate that, by the end of this year, we will have saved more than $100,000 in medical insurance premiums over the past three years! That money has been used to bring on two more part-time employees, send one of our Elders into foreign missions, pay down our church's mortgage, and increase other elements of employee compensation.

Personally, it has added a new level of complexity to how I balance my pastoral income, but I haven't minded. Our church has worked with us on making sure that their desire to provide for us financially through raises or increased benefits is done in such a way that it does not affect our MAGI any more than absolutely necessary.

All in all, it has been a true blessing.

Chapter 2
Considerations

Now that you've read our story, I'd like to focus in on certain key issues that we had to consider before making this decision OR have had to continue considering each year since.

Understanding Pastoral Compensation

When I talk about pastoral compensation, I am referring to the totality of a pastor's income and all employee benefits which he receives. These things are, obviously, either decided upon by the church at the time he is hired, or developed over time as the church's ability to provide them for its pastor grows.

Furthermore, when I refer to pastoral income, I am referring to the combination of a pastor's base salary and his housing allowance. The church is responsible for setting the overall amount of the pastor's income, but only the pastor can determine what amount of that income will be designated as salary and what amount will be designated as housing allowance.[9]

---

[9] This is practically correct, but technically incorrect. Technically, a pastor is supposed to submit a designation request of some sort to the church indicating how much of his income he wants to be designated as housing allowance. The church (or a governing body within the church) must then approve that designation. However, practically speaking, it has been my observation that churches usually approve whatever is

Balancing Salary and Housing Allowance

For churches considering dropping all medical coverage for their pastors so that they can get coverage through one of the Obamacare exchanges, it is critical that they understand that all premium and cost savings subsidies are directly based on the MAGI of the pastor.

Since, in a pastor's case, his MAGI will likely only include his salary and not his housing allowance, it is critical that he finds the right balance between these two numbers.

That means that a pastor inadvertently choosing to set his housing allowance too high or too low could have a drastic effect on how much he pays for health coverage.

However, unlike pretty much every other employee in the world, pastors have the ability to control, via their housing allowance designation, how much MAGI they end up reporting at tax time.

This balance will need to be re-examined on a yearly basis.

Timing

Since it is possible that a pastor's family may be subject to a time-consuming Medicaid review like our family was, every effort should be made to submit an application for coverage through the healthcare.gov website (or similar state exchange) as soon as possible once open enrollment begins.[10]

---

submitted by the pastor since the pastor alone will be accountable for that designation at tax time.

[10] For 2017, that will be November 1.

Having said that, technically, a church could create a situation so that the employee qualifies for a special enrollment period by setting a date for the end of church-provided medical coverage earlier in the year.

In our case, we chose to stick with the normal enrollment period because it fit more naturally into our budget calendar.

Regardless, pastors should give themselves as much lead time as possible in order to navigate a Medicaid review so that their children do not experience a gap of coverage.

Choosing a Plan
While premium subsidies are available on any plan, cost-sharing subsidies are only available on Silver plans. In order to get the maximum savings, you will be required to choose a Silver plan in order for the benefits described above to apply to you.[11]

Getting Counsel/Advice
The best thing we did was to get professional counsel from a CPA about our specific situation . . . both from the church's perspective and

---

[11] Health insurance plans offered through healthcare.gov or a similar state exchange will fall into one of four "metal" categories: Bronze, Silver, Gold, or Platinum. If you were to receive no subsidy at all, Bronze plans would be the cheapest and Platinum plans would be the most expensive. If your MAGI is within 400% of the federal poverty level, you may qualify for a premium subsidy (a.k.a premium tax credit). In addition, if your MAGI is within 250% of the federal poverty level, you may also qualify for the cost-sharing subsidy which can significantly reduce your out-of-pocket expense limits . . . as long as you choose a Silver plan. Cost-sharing subsidies are only available on Silver plans.

from each pastor's perspective. If you choose to go down this path, you must do the same.

Increasing Compensation Over Time

Since the balance between my salary and housing allowance is now so critical to the amount of premium and cost-sharing subsidies I receive, any increases to my income can be a problem.

In my case, I have reached a point where receiving additional income could become detrimental to the balance between my salary and housing allowance. Since I have maxed out my reasonable housing allowance designation, any additional income I receive automatically counts as salary.

This leaves both the church and I with one primary option each. If the church is determined to give me a raise in my income, then the only way I can offset the effect of that raise is by increasing contributions to my own personal traditional IRA.

Money contributed to a traditional IRA is deducted from total income and is, therefore, not counted towards my MAGI. So, if the church wants to give me a $1,000 raise in income next year, I can simply contribute that same amount to my IRA, and it will be as if the raise never happened at all. It will have no effect on my Obamacare subsidies.

A similar, but slightly different approach is that, in lieu of increasing my income, the church could simply increase their contribution to my

SEP IRA.[12] Contributions made to a SEP on my behalf have no impact on my reportable income. It allows the church to increase my compensation without increasing my taxable income.

Obviously, both methods have the same end – increasing retirement assets for a pastor's future care.

NON-PASTORAL EMPLOYEES
In our case, our church does not employ any full-time, non-pastoral employees, nor did we ever provide health insurance coverage for any part-time employees. So, in our case, dropping medical coverage was easy because the only employees affected were the ones who would actually benefit.

If your church has full-time, non-pastoral employees who currently receive medical insurance coverage from your church, please know that if the church decides to drop medical coverage, it has to be for all employees.

Unfortunately, unlike pastors, non-pastoral employees will not have the various benefits that pastors have in structuring their income so as to maximize premium and cost-sharing subsidies. This reality must be taken into account, and these employees must be cared for.

---

[12] To understand why I believe that a SEP IRA is the best retirement plan for churches to offer to pastors, see Chapter 6 in *Structuring Pastoral Compensation* or Chapter 6 in *How to Not Be a Broke Pastor*.

Chapter 3
Final Thoughts

Should you do what we did? I honestly cannot say. Every church and every pastor are so unique that there is no one-size-fits-all answer to this question. All I have endeavored to do here is to show you what we have experienced and to help you think through the things we had to consider.

To be honest, we didn't really want to go down the path we have chosen. What we wanted was to keep the plan we originally had at the price we were originally paying. However, that option was taken away from us, and over time, the church was priced out of the market in terms of providing medical insurance for our pastors on our own. For us, in a sense, we very much felt that we were forced down this path by the implementation of the Affordable Care Act.

Whatever decision you arrive at, or whatever choice you make, I know that your church is feeling these same pressures. May God give you wisdom and grace as you seek to care for your pastors in the best manner possible.

Visit www.brokepastor.com, the #1 online resource for understanding pastoral compensation and finance issues, for more topics, information, and resources that you can use.

Don't be a **BROKE PASTOR**

Are you struggling to understand the unique and challenging world of pastoral compensation? Are you maximizing the benefits that could be yours by simply being "wise as a serpent and innocent as a dove" when it comes to how you structure your pastoral pay?

As a pastor, I get it. Not only can our compensation be confusing, but there are also so many different components that need to be balanced . . . it can be hard to put all the pieces together.

How to Not Be a Broke Pastor is written for pastors/ministers and is designed to make the complexities of clergy pay simple and easy to understand, and also to give you ideas as to how you can use your income to the greatest extent possible.

Bless Your Pastor!

Is your church structuring its pastoral compensation package in a way that truly blesses your pastor? Is your church doing all it can and should to financially provide for the pastors who keep watch over your souls?

The fact of the matter is that too many churches have never given any thought to what a pastoral compensation package should look like, and much less to how they should structure it so that their pastor receives the maximum benefit.

Structuring Pastoral Compensation is written for church decision makers (Elders, Deacons, Trustees, Committee Members, etc.) to help them understand what should be included in their pastor's compensation and how to best implement the various pieces so that their pastor will be truly blessed.

Learn to invest from the *Pros*!

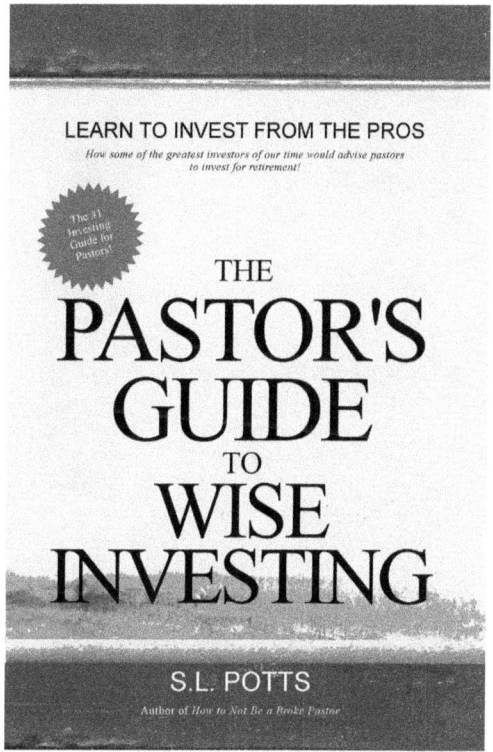

Pastors are so good at so many difficult things - preaching/teaching, counseling, discipling, caring - but can very often be completely clueless when it comes to handling their money wisely. This can be true of their day-to-day finances, but is often more true in regards to their retirement planning.

The Pastor's Guide to Wise Investing takes the, often, confusing world of investing and makes it simple and easy to understand by compiling and condensing the best advice from the best investors of our day into one simple, easy-to-read guide.

www.ingramcontent.com/pod-product-compliance
Lightning Source LLC
Chambersburg PA
CBHW070756050426
42452CB00010B/1865